North Florida Roads with Stories on the Side

J. Kent Thompson

©2017 J. Kent Thompson. All rights reserved
ISBN 978-1-365-82804-1

Copies can be ordered from the publisher at:
www.lulu.com\shop\

1st Edition

Why This Book?

Florida started as a land covered by Indian trails that eventually became plank roads, then dirt roads, country roads, highways and city streets. All lead to some special place with a story that needs to be told. In this book I share stories of the history of north Florida.

Be it the largest real estate deal in Florida history, long forgotten beach hotels, confederate salt works, lighthouses, or cemeteries, they are what make up the patch-work quilt we call north Florida.

You are invited to travel a few roads with me and learn of Sulphur springs, mullet runs, volcanos, and one-eyed preachers. In doing so, I hope to rekindle your memories or spark an interest in exploring north Florida and its history.

Table of Contents

Before the Roads--- Indians and Spaniards	1
The Forbes Purchase and the Forgotten Coast	11
Sheriff of the Seafood Industry	21
I Shot the Deputy	29
The One-eyed Preacher who became Governor	39
Tungston Plantation	53
Sulphur Springs in North Florida	57
The Hampton Springs Hotel	59
The Wakulla Beach Hotel	65
The Seine Yards	67
My Mullet Can Fly?	71
The Wakulla Volcano	75
Confederate Salt Works	87
Ed Ball and the Wakulla Springs Lodge	91
The Union Bank	95
I Ain't Got No Body!	97
The Nautilus Center	103

1

Before the Roads---Indians and Spaniards

Florida was first discovered and settled by the Paleo-Indians. They had migrated across the Bering Straits into North America and gradually began settling across the continent some 14,000 years ago. The land we now know as Florida was called *Ikanayuska* and later *Cautio*.

By the 1500s there were five main people groups in Florida. The Apalachee in Northern Florida, the Timucuan in Northeast Florida, the Tocobaga in central Florida, the Calusa in Southwest Florida, and the Tequesta in Southeast Florida.

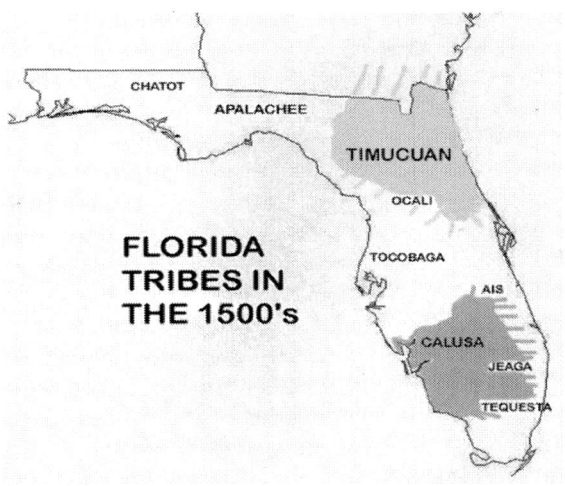

Major Indian Tribes in Florida

The tribes evolved into highly developed cultures and communities. The Apalachee were successful farmers of what would become known as the "three sisters crop" of corn, beans and squash. The Calusa were fishers, adept at netting and curing fish for trade in Cuba. The Tequesta were also known as ocean-going traders. The Timucuan had highly developed societies spanning 15 different villages, all speaking a common language. It was these tribes that met the first white men to come to what was to become known as Florida's shores.

Indian lore tells how the white man first appeared in their land. Many years ago, great salt waves broke upon the shoreline leaving a long line of white foam on the sand. When the sun came out it melted the foam and in its place stood armed men. The sun glistened off their helmets and swords. They stopped, looked back at the sea, then walked into the forests and disappeared.
No doubt these were the Spanish Conquistadores. One such Conquistador, Juan Ponce de Leon would claim the land for his Spanish King in 1513. He renamed it "la Florida" in honor of Pascua Florida his homeland Easter celebration of the flowers. The Calusa Indians would return the favor by killing him in his 1521 return visit to their shores.

Flag of the King of Spain

Soon more white men came, this time in great ships the Indians called large birds with white wings. Their inhabitant's goals were to find riches rumored to be plentiful in this new land, capture Indian slaves to work in their South American mines, and lastly to spread Christianity. It's ironic how the first two goals had nothing to do with the last. While they were not successful in finding material wealth, they did manage to decimate the aboriginal Indian populations through forced slavery and their European diseases.

Each ship brought hopeful settlers but the harsh environment and local Indians saw many perish. It was not until 1565 that the first permanent settlement was established in Saint Augustine. The Spanish saw Florida as a useful possession, especially along the east and west coasts where the Gulf stream waters flowed. Spain established two strongholds in the new land, one in St. Augustine and the other in Pensacola. They then went about building forts and missions throughout northern Florida up into the Carolinas. By controlling eastern and western Florida they could better protect their treasure laden ships traveling the Gulf stream to Cuba. Spain controlled Florida for the next 250 years.

In 1763 Spain traded Florida to the British who in return gave them back the city of Havana, Cuba captured during their Seven Years War.

British Florida

Union Flag of Great Britain

The British took control of Florida in 1763 and would rule it for the next twenty years. The British governed differently than Spain. They established two colonies, East Florida and West Florida, their 14th and 15th colonies in America and moved to develop an export economy verses the Spanish agrarian model.

They recognized British traders and loyalists, Willliam Panton, Thomas Forbes, and John Leslie, who had started a company called the *Panton, Leslie and Company* with brother John Forbes as their business manager. Paton and Leslie traded with the Indians but much of their trade was credit.

St. Augustine became the capital of East Florida and Pensacola the capital of West Florida. These two colonies remained loyal to Britain during the American Revolutionary War. Spain, which had indirectly supported France, America's ally, captured the city of Pensacola in 1781 and held it throughout the war. When the 1783 Treaty of Paris ended the Revolutionary War, Britain abandoned all of Florida to the control of Spain. British loyalists *Panton, Leslie and Company* remained as agents for the Indians on behalf of the Spanish.

National Flag of Spain

Spain took over Florida with a different attitude in 1783. They lured Spanish citizens to the area with promises of land grants. They also welcomed American settlers to settle the lands if they signed a loyalty oath to the Spanish.

Another group also came to Florida seeking refuge and freedom—black slaves from southern plantations and Lower Creek Indians from Alabama seeking refuge. These refugees and runaways would later be called *Seminoles*. In an act of friendship and cooperation Spain entered into a treaty with the U.S. called *Pinckney's Treaty* or the *Treaty of San Lorenzo* in October of 1795. Both sides agreed to a southern boundary for Florida, to protect navigation on its waters, and not incite the native Indians to warfare.

The *Paton and Leslie Company* continued to trade with the Indians, and as British Loyalists, they were more than willing to provide them with guns and ammunition to fight the Americans.

By 1804 the *Paton and Leslie Company* requested payment from the Indians for all debts as well as losses from theft during Indian raids on their trading posts. In a May 25, 1804 meeting at the Indian village of Cheskatalafa, twenty-four Seminole and Lower Creek Chiefs agreed to transfer 1.2 million acres of land along the Apalachicola River to the company now called *John Forbes & Company* in exchange of cash payments of debts. This land transfer was approved by the Spanish government with the stipulation no land transferred would be sold to the Americans. The sale became known as the Forbes Purchase. Three smaller adjacent tracts of land would be added to the original tract in 1811.

Relations between the United States and England deteriorated into war in 1812. Many British loyalists sought refuge in Florida. The *John Forbes and Company*, continued to support the Indian and British efforts against the United States. To curb their influence, the U.S. sought to open trading posts above the Florida line. The British, to protect their interests in the North Florida area (even though it was owned by Spain) built a fort 15 miles above the mouth of the Apalachicola River near a Forbes trading post at Prospect Bluff. It was alternately known as the British Post or Fort, Prospect Bluff Fort, and Nicolls Fort after its commander. Built to support their Creek Indian allies it was later abandoned and taken over by runaway slaves. This resulted in the fort later being called the "*Negro Fort.*" The fort soon became a thorn in the side of ships navigating the river who came under constant attack from its inhabitants.

In 1816 the U.S. sent Colonel Clinch to lead an expedition into Florida against the Negro Fort. He attacked the fort and while bombarding it, a hot shot cannonball landed in the fort's powder room. It blew the fort apart, killing some 270 of the 320 men, women, and children inside the fort.

The John Forbes Company, sensing the weakness of the Spanish position, and the eventual transfer of Florida to the U.S. decided to sell its holdings rather than try to negotiate a fair price with the Americans. In October of 1817 Forbes sold the land to Colin Mitchel, a Havana, Cuba merchant who held American, English and Spanish citizenship for approximately $135,000.00.

The influx of settlers and runaways coming into Florida from the Americas soon became too much for the Spanish to handle. Slave owners came seeking their runaways and the Indians preyed on the settlers both in Florida and the neighboring states of Georgia and Alabama. The new American government demanded Spain police their problems as agreed in the *Pinckney Treaty*, but ruling from afar, they could not. Spain had become embroiled in further armed conflicts in Europe and South America and could not spare soldiers to protect their possessions in Florida.

Due to the increased hostilities of the Seminole Indians in Florida, General Andrew Jackson was ordered in 1818 to take the fight to the Indians in

Florida. He destroyed the Seminole village of Mikasuki. then marched on to Fowl Town on the Suwannee River and then St. Marks, taking possession of both. At Fowl Town he captured Robert Ambrister a former British solider under Nicolls command. At St. Marks he captured Alexander Arbuthnot a Scotch trader. Jackson accused the men of inciting the Indian hostilities and sentenced both to death. Jackson then crossed the Apalachicola River and marched on West Florida where he captured Pensacola.

The governments of England and Spain were not happy with Jackson's actions. The U.S. Senate was called to investigate the matter and to censure Jackson. The forts and cities were quickly returned to Spain, and England did not press the case of its subject's deaths. President Madison, whom many said supported Jackson's efforts, refused to censure him.

The eventual transfer of Florida to the U.S. can be directly tied to Jackson's actions. If Spain wanted to hold on to their possession, they would have to commit manpower and money to maintain a large military force, something they could not afford to do. Sensing weakness on Spain's part and wanting to secure its southern coasts, the Americans told Spain to protect its citizens or trade the land to the United States. After negotiations with U.S. Secretary of State John Quincy Adams, Spain agreed to cede Florida to the U.S. In return the Americans agreed to pay restitution claims of Florida citizens against Spain up to a sum of five million dollars, the U.S. also agreed to give up any claims to Texas.

The 1845 U.S. Flag with 23 Stars

To look after its citizens and landholders the Spanish government stipulated that all properties given in land grants prior to the Treaty ratification be honored. To honor such a request would have meant that most of Florida would still be held by Spanish citizens.

The U.S. resisted this stipulation for to not do so would leave in place the Alagon, Punonrosto and Vagas land grants, the three largest in Florida. Instead the U.S. agreed to only honor any grants made before the negotiations with Spain had begun, January 24, 1818. This date invalidated the Alagon, Punonrosto and Vagas land grants. While this resulted in favor to the U.S. who looked to sell the lands, they overlooked one big tract of land, the Forbes Purchase.

Spain formally transferred Florida to the United States through the Adams-Onis Treaty in 1821.

2

The Forbes Purchase and the Forgotten Coast

The 1804 Forbes Purchase was the largest land grant in Florida history. It encompassed 1.5 million acres of land between the Wakulla and Apalachicola Rivers and included the gulf barrier islands to the south and reached as far north as Tallahassee.

This land was one to become, through the years, one of the most valuable properties in north Florida. From its boundaries came what we currently call the *forgotten coast* with its barrier islands of St. George, Dog, St. Vincent, Cape San Blas, and St. James as well as the cities of Apalachicola, St. Joseph, Carrabelle, Sopchoppy, Crawfordville, St. Marks, Newport, Woodville, Blountstown, and Tallahassee. The history of north Florida beats within this heartland.

A map of the area today would show it encompassed the northwestern part of Leon County, southern portion of Gadsden County, all of Franklin & Wakulla Counties, and all but the northern tip of Liberty County. It was unique in the fact that it was the only land grant made by Native Americans that was ever upheld by the U.S. Supreme Court.

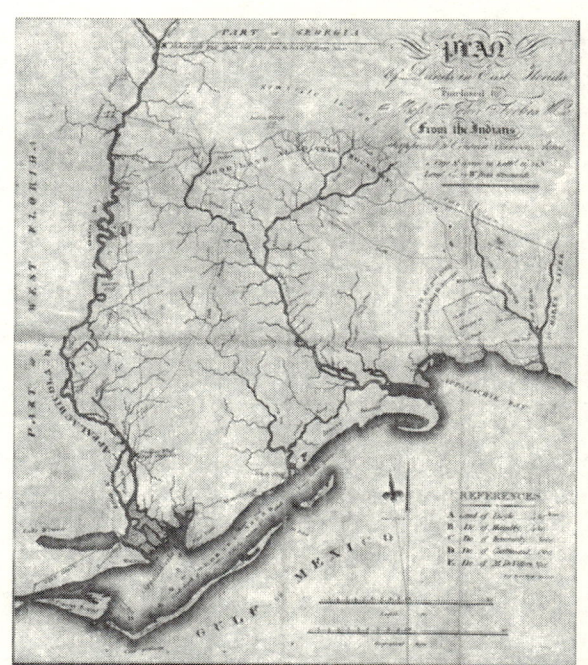

Map of the Forbes Purchase from the state Archives of Florida

In Florida's transfer to the U.S. it had noted in Article 8 of the Adams-Onis Treaty that:

All the grants of land made before the 24th of January 1818 by His Catholic Majesty or by his lawful authorities in the said Territories ceded by His Majesty to the United States shall be ratified and confirmed to the persons in possession of the lands, <u>to the same extent that the same grants would be valid if the territories had remained under the dominion of His Catholic Majesty</u>.

The problem with this clause was it contradicted by an 1823 Supreme Court ruling. In *Johnson v. McIntosh* the court had ruled that Indians who had sold land to individuals in Indiana in 1773 and 1775, had no right to sell the land. While they could possess it for their use, the European "discovery" of America had automatically divested them of the power to dispose of the soil at their own will to whomever they pleased. This "discovery doctrine" basically said the land they had long inhabited was now owned by the European discoverers. When England had been in possession of Florida from 1763-83, King George had made a similar ruling. In his Royal Proclamation of 1763 he barred the purchase of native lands without England's "especial leave and license for that purpose first obtained."

Spain regained sovereignty over Florida in 1783 through the Treaty of Paris. Spain subsequently signed a 1784 Treaty in Pensacola with the Seminole and Talpuche Indians that promised them "*the security and guarantee of those lands which they hold, according to the right of property with which they possessed them, on condition that they are comprehended within the lines and limits of His Catholic Majesty.*"

For the next fourteen years, Colin Mitchel and his associates would argue with bureaucrats, legislators, Governors and judges that the Forbes Purchase was a valid grant that must be upheld by the United States, pursuant to Article 8 of the Adams-Onis Treaty.

The validity of the purchase was first questioned by an 1824 board of land commissioners, and then rejected by an 1830 territorial court in Florida. The case was appealed to the U.S. Supreme Court who postponed hearing it for the next five years.

In 1835 the court heard the case and the owners' rights to the Forbes Purchase was upheld in *Mitchel v United States*. The verdict was based upon the Spanish governments approval and confirmation of the Forbes Purchase when it had occurred. In its ruling the court removed that portion of their claim to the territory adjacent to the fort at St. Marks stating it was the property of the United States. It was only because of this ruling that the fort and the city of St. Marks has been preserved in Florida history.

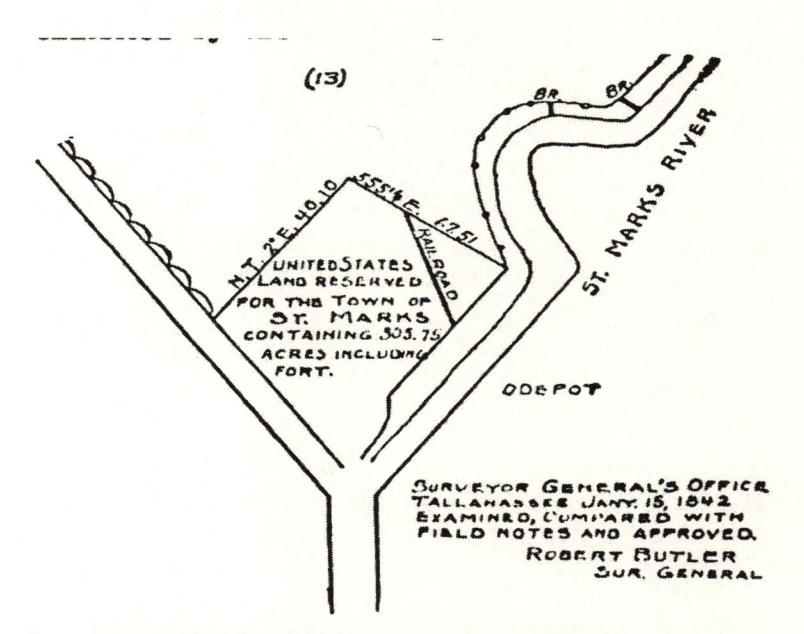

Survey reserving land for St. Marks and Fort San Marcos de Apalache from the Forbes Purchase

After the ruling, the *Forbes Company* was reorganized as the *Apalachicola Land Company*. What began next was the first of many Florida land booms.

An assessment of their holdings revealed four types of land: hammocks, pine land, swamp and marsh. Only two parcels in the tract were identified as fertile and suitable for agriculture, one along the northern boundary adjacent to Little River and the other on the west bank of the Wakulla River. Later surveys would identify Ochlockonee Bay as a future city site due to its deep-water entrance. Also noted was Shell Point and the springs and sinkholes in the area. It was said that due to its excellent fishing and healthful air it would be advantageous for sea-bathing and as a summer retreat during the "sickly season." It was felt that the land east of the Ochlockonee River had abundant timber resources while the land west of the river had little potential value.

The first four years of sales proved profitable, resulting in the migration of large populations of settlers and a booming local commerce only rivaled by New Orleans, and Mobile. Many of the new arrivals came from Georgia, Alabama, and the Carolina's.

The Beginnings of Apalachicola

Before the *Apalachicola Land Company* could begin selling their land around Apalachicola, they had to deal with squatters. While the company owners had fought in court for their title to the Forbes Purchase land, others had moved onto the property and constructed business's and dwellings with no title at all.

What was to become Apalachicola had its start as an Indian village. In 1705 the Spanish built a fort at the mouth of the Apalachicola River but the areas were sparsely inhabited. In the 1750s the area served as a hideout for pirates preying on Spanish treasure ships. Late in the 1700s a trading post was established on Murder Point (today known as 10 Foot Hole). The area became known as Cotton Town, then Cottonton. When the U.S. took possession of Florida in 1822, the area began to grow. In 1828 the town was incorporated as West Point and then renamed Apalachicola in 1831. When Franklin County was formed from what had been part of Jackson County, Apalachicola became the county seat. By 1835 Apalachicola was the third largest port on the Gulf of Mexico.

With the 1835 ruling upholding the Forbes Purchase, many in Apalachicola thought their claims to the Forbes land would be grandfathered in and they would be granted titles. But this was not the case. The *Apalachicola Land Company* found a city that had been laid out haphazardly and decided to develop a plan for the town. Although they give first preference to the residents living on the land, many squatters decided to leave rather than pay the prices the company was asking. A street layout mirroring the city of Philadelphia was instituted and the channel from the anchorage to the riverfront wharves was deepened. To protect from fire, business buildings were required to be constructed of brick. To further development, the company donated the streets, squares and a lot for construction of a courthouse.

Disgruntled former citizens decided to move outside the boundaries of the *Apalachicola Land Company* holdings to St. Joseph's Bay. They formed the city of St. Joseph in 1836 to compete for the river commerce of Apalachicola.

St. Joseph

Blessed with a deep-water port the city soon prospered. To compete with Apalachicola the merchants of St. Joseph decided to build a railroad higher up the Apalachicola River from Lake Wimico to the Bay. This would allow them by-pass Apalachicola. Because the lake was too shallow for deep draft steamboats to pass, a new city called Iona was built at the river terminus of the railroad that reached from there to the Bay. The rail line from St. Joseph to Iona was opened in 1839 becoming Florida's first steam-powered railroad.

The city was a quick success and soon became known as a resort for tourists. To promote its tourism race tracks, gambling houses, and houses of ill- repute sprang up and with them a reputation as a wicked and immoral place followed. Visitors included Florida's Governor and legislators as well as the idle rich. In 1838 Florida's Constitutional Convention was held in St. Joseph's not because of its southern charm but its reputation. Success is sometimes a fleeting visitor and for St. Joseph this proved to be true. In 1841 a yellow fever epidemic devastated the population and those who survived moved away, some even dismantling homes and moving them back to Apalachicola. In 1844 a major hurricane with huge tidal waters destroyed what was left of the town. Today St. Joseph is but a ghost town of graves.

Apalachicola continued to be a major port only to begin its decline after the Civil War with the construction of more railways that created faster, more efficient means to transport goods.

Timber, naval stores, and commercial fishing, coupled with tourism were always prevalent in the area and would become the basis of the future economies.

The seafood industry has always been a mainstay in Franklin County but the oyster industry has been the most successful. It was a 1913 law establishing the Florida Shell Fish Commission that gave the state the right to lease submerged lands and plant oysters that got the attention of the *Apalachicola Land Company* and landed the Forbes Purchase back in court.

Back in Court

In 1923 The Apalachicola Land Company sued Agriculture Commissioner W.A. McRae over the ownership of submerged lands under navigable and tide waters in Apalachicola Bay. The company alleged they owned the water bottoms as granted under the Supreme Court ruling of 1835. The state claimed they were exercising authority under the Florida Riparian Act of 1856 which gave them title below the high-water mark. The *Apalachicola Land Company* countered claiming title to the water bottoms was part of their land grant. The court studied the applicable laws of Spain and England when they were in control of the land and could not find any instance where the rights to navigable waters were granted to individuals. It held that the rights to public use were always reserved by the sovereign and found that the state, not the *Apalachicola Land Company* owned the submerged water bottoms.

Today most of the undeveloped lands of what was the Forbes Purchase are either within the Apalachicola National Forest or owned by the St. Joe Paper Company.

3

Sheriff of the Seafood Industry

The Shell Fish Commission was created June 4, 1913 by the Florida legislature to "encourage, protect, regulate, and develop the shell fish industry of the State of Florida." Shell fish were defined as oysters, clams, and whelks. The act declared state ownership of water bottoms and oyster and clam reefs. It created the office of Shell Fish Commissioner and defined his powers. It allowed for the leasing of oyster and clam beds to either Florida residents or corporations legally authorized to do business in the state, limiting the leases to 500 acres per lessee, the licensing and registration of vessels employed in the industry and levied a tax on production of shellfish. It also repealed all laws on the same subject matter or those in conflict with it.

The new law placed the Commission under the Commissioner of Agriculture, (Mr. W. A. McRae, 1912-23), (Mr. Nathan Mayo 1923-60). The Shell Fish Commissioner was to be appointed by the Governor. Mr. T. R. (Texas Ruff) Hodges, "a man of energy and discretion" was appointed by Governor Trammel as the first secretary of the Shell Fish Commission.

T. R. Hodges

T. R. Texas Ruff (pronounced "roof") Hodges, the tenth of eleven children, was born in Florida on Hickory Island in 1874. He was the son of Dr. and Mrs. Andrew Elton Hodges, a pioneer family of Levy County Florida. He married Ethel Mobley of South Carolina on October 4, 1905. They had one child Robert Randolph who was born October 19, 1912. Hodges attended the East Florida Seminary in Gainesville and served as a U. S. Navy Captain in World War I.

Newspaper accounts of Hodges stated that upon assuming the job of Shell Fish Commissioner in 1913, he had "for many years been engaged in the oyster business and so is well acquainted of all the details." Anecdotal information show's that Hodges was reported to be particular about his appearance, wearing a sparkling white uniform, sometimes changing clothes several times a day to maintain his image. While serving as Shell Fish Commissioner he was accused of high living at the expense of the state, acting like a European monarch and affecting an attitude of disdain for the fishermen.

Shell Fish Commissioner T.R. Hodges

Hodges held U.S. Steamboat Masters papers and served as Captain of the Shell Fish Commission's first patrol vessel the yacht "*Seafoam*" and later a 94 ft. steam yacht "*The Roamer*", the 110 ft. converted sub-chaser "S.C. 144", and the 160 ft. "*USS Dispatch*" on his inspections along the coasts of the state. He also maintained an office on board the vessels.

Besides serving as Florida's first Shell Fish Commissioner, he later worked in the newspaper business in Cedar Key, Bronson, Starke and Jacksonville. He also operated an insurance agency and practiced law in Cedar Key for 30 years. Hodges lived a colorful life, always interjecting himself into the current events of the day as well as establishing himself as the Hodges family historian. It seemed anytime he could get someone's ear (especially a reporter's) he took every opportunity to speak of his and his families past. Some accounts, when studied show conflicting information however, that throws some caution to the reader as to the veracity of the information. One story Hodges told in later years recalled how he had led the charge to defeat a leper colony in Cedar Key in 1921. He ran unsuccessfully for Secretary of State in 1930. Hodges died in 1962.

The Early Years of the Shell Fish Commission

The 1913 law had vested Hodges with the authority to appoint deputies as constituted police officers to act as his collectors and patrolmen. The deputies were paid $50.00 a month and were appointed for one year with their terms expiring April 15th of each year.

He was authorized to purchase boats, vessels and other property necessary to regulate and control the oyster and clam industry. He was also granted authority to establish patrols of the waters and if necessary to use force to capture violators.

Hodges proposed twenty-five rules that were adopted by the Commissioner of Agriculture. The first eight concerned the conduct of the Deputy Shell Fish Commissioners in doing their job and dealing with the fishing community. The rest of the rules gave the commissioner the authority to close shellfish beds when deemed necessary, to sell leased water bottoms for non-payment of annual rental, required proper licensing, set a three inch size limit for oysters (dealers were provided with a standard size measure by the Commissioner bearing his official seal to use to measure their catch), required the return of shucked shells to the bar, granted authority to seize boats and cargos, and to issue permits to take oysters during the closed season from April 15 until October 1 of each year for bedding purposes.

Deputies also served as collectors, collecting a weekly two cents per barrel tax on oysters or clams in the shell, and one cent per gallon on opened oysters or clams, a $2.00 police license on shell-stock dealers, a $5.00 license on half shell dealers, a fifty cent per acre rental fee per year for leases (which expired after ten years or the fee was upped to one dollar per acre) and an annual boat license fee equal to fifty cents per ton of the vessels carrying capacity.

Deputies were to see to it that every boat engaged in the oyster industry had the proper license and had their registration number painted on each side of the bow in figures six inches long. There were 14 original Deputy Shell Fish Commissioners appointed by Mr. Hodges. By 1916 this number had increased to 21 officers. Monies collected were deposited in local bank accounts established by the Agriculture Commissioner

Evidently Hodges had impressed his deputies of his seriousness about his new job, as the Commission showed a surplus to the state treasury each year from revenues collected. This surprised many, coming from an organization that was not expected to be in the black for two or three years.

One of the first things Commissioner Hodges did upon taking office was to conduct a physical survey of the fisheries of the state, traveling along the coast from Fernandina to Pensacola. At each stop he met with the fishing interests and discussed the new "fish law" he also issued a letter to the local newspapers concerning his efforts and the state of the oyster industry.

In letters submitted to the *Fishing Gazette*, he lamented the fact that "what can be built into one of the States greatest industries and be made to yield a tremendous income is rapidly being completely ruined." Hodges noted that along the east coast many cities were dumping raw sewage in the inland canals that resulted in the killing of shellfish as well as creating health risks and issued orders for people to install septic tanks to "do away with the nuisance at small cost."

He stated that the new shellfish law was "about 15 years too late to save the once magnificent natural oyster beds of the state, which have been depleted by the constant drain upon them without any restriction." Hodges found that the bars of the east and west coasts had been swept clean by dredges and in some instances even the clutch, which provided future oysters, removed. He deplored the depletion of the oyster beds in St. Andrews due to "constant tonging, in and out of season."

He wrote that "the beautifully paved streets of Apalachicola, Fernandina, St. Augustine and other cities of the east coast together with the fine country roads of Duval and other counties, constructed of oyster shells, are tombstones to the departed oyster industry of the State of Florida." He called for the shells to be replaced on the bars to stop "killing the goose that laid the golden egg." Despite all of the conditions he had noted Hodges was optimistic that the future could be bright, writing "if the Shellfish Commission received the hearty cooperation of the people of Florida, I believe within four years the industry will grow…and our once magnificent industry will be restored."

Added Responsibilities Include the entire Fishery

In 1915 the legislature, in response to Hodges proposals and his successful efforts, expanded the duties of the Commissioner to include all saltwater fish, shrimp, crawfish, crabs and sponge. Many of the laws passed then are applicable today. One of the most controversial was the ownership of the state's water bottoms.

Shellfish Commissioner Hodges policed the fish and oyster industry on board his 64-foot yacht named the "*Seafoam*". The vessel had two 25 horsepower 4-cylinder gas engines and was capable of traveling at speeds of 9 to 11 knots. Charles Duckwall of Sarasota was Captain of the "*Seafoam*" and his son Charles Duckwall Jr. served as the engineer. There were also three smaller vessels available for the deputies; by 1916 the fleet had increased to 22 vessels.

Initial enforcement efforts were confined to the coast. Officers would travel around their areas, camping out in tents or sleeping aboard their boat if one were assigned. A majority of the work was carried out in conjunction with the Commissioners vessel as it had sleeping quarters, and a galley. Commissioner Hodges enforced the laws with a passion viewing himself, as he said in 1916 as "practically a Sheriff for the entire state of Florida." His strict enforcement of seasonal restrictions and legal methods of fishing had resulted he claimed, "In more demand for oysters, cheaper market prices, and better quality."

Fishers verses Enforcers: The Battle Line is Drawn

Commercial fishermen however, took a different view of all these new regulations and Hodges enforcement practices. Calling him "Commodore Hodges," the fishermen disliked his authoritative manner when dealing with them. They felt he acted like he was above them, having no interest in their welfare. They had three main objections to the new conservation policies and laws. First they felt that any restrictions on their trade were unnecessary, as up to this time fishing was considered a *"pastime"* instead of an occupation. Second, to finance the Commissioner and his department the state had levied fees on the catches, boats, leases, and dealers. Lastly they were angered by the purchase of a 94 ft boat named "*The Roamer*" from John K. Robinson of New York which was being used to patrol the Gulf Coast. They also riled against the deputies boarding their vessels and seizing their catches and equipment, which were destroyed upon conviction.

Animosities had intensified to such an extent that an armed clash had broken out over an oyster lease in Southport, Fl where Deputy Shellfish Commissioner Moses Dykes, trying to make an arrest, was killed by John Cannon, a local commercial fisherman.

4

I Shot the Deputy

It was in 1915, just a year and a half after the Shellfish Commission was organized that an officer was murdered in Southport, Florida. Deputy Shellfish Moses John Dykes was the first and *only* officer ever violently killed in the line of duty while protecting the marine resources of Florida.

Shellfish Commissioner, T.R. Hodges knew when he took the job that he had his hands full. He had been asked to create a police force over the natural resources of the state. He was told to appoint his officers and have them go out and collect tax money on the taking of oysters. The only problem was none of the fishermen felt that they needed the regulations. As far as they and many other in the state were concerned, fishing was a right, not a business or industry.

In 1914, the state had passed rules requiring oystermen to purchase leases to harvest oysters off the traditional oyster beds. A limited few had been granted permits to work the beds and this was the beginning of a decades old controversy that would be played out many times between the haves and the have-nots, unfortunately it would also place the Shellfish Commission and her successors right in the middle.

In Southport, the tradition of fishing is as strong today as it was hundreds of years ago. The people had a fierce pride in what they did and a strong sense of independence to go with it. They did not like anyone telling them what they could or could not do, or where they could or could not go. For years' fishermen merely went out in their front yards — the bays, streams, inlets and gulf to ply their trade. They took what they wanted or needed and never had to worry if it would be there tomorrow. Their main concern was that the weather allowed them to do what they loved most, fish.

With the creation of the Shellfish Commission, things were beginning to change, or at least someone in the person of T.R. Hodges was trying to make it change. Fishermen gathered at their usual meeting places, the fish houses, the coffee shops and the boat ramps and grumbled about the new Commissioner and his taxes and regulations. They argued that the state had no right to regulate them and especially not to grant leases to a chosen few and run them off their oyster beds. An enterprising "jack-leg preacher" from Chicago by the name of C.T. Anderson had formed a partnership with a local named Jim Youngblood, and together they had bought the leases for most of North Bay. The Southport fishermen were furious that vast oyster beds where they normally tonged oysters had been leased out.

Big John Cannon was one of these fishermen. Described as someone who had little education but lots of courage, he was known as a fearless man not even "afraid of the devil." He had moved his family to Sheepshead Bayou in Southport in 1901 and he earned his living tonging the big, sweet Southport oysters in North Bay. He was not used to anyone telling him what to do and some Commissioner in Tallahassee or anywhere else was not going to start now. He had spent his life on the sea. It was rumored that he had served on the "Maine" and was aboard her when it was sunk in Havana, Cuba but records of the Maine survivors do not support the rumor.

Wearing a recognizable black Stetson hat, everyone knew when John Cannon was on the water. He had watched as the leases had been posted and had decided that no one was going to stop him from oystering anywhere he damned well pleased. He and several other oystermen just chose to ignore the signs, as far as they were concerned, they might be able to post them, but they weren't going to be able to stop them from oystering.

Friday January 8, 1915 looked like a good day to go on the bay to Big John Cannon. He loaded up his boat and his 12-year-old son Junie and headed out to the posted beds of North Bay. That same morning, Shellfish Commission officers Moses John Dykes and R.D. Gilbert armed with a warrant for Cannon's arrest set sail on North Bay. Piloting the officer's boat was Roland Mason, a local, who took them to Alligator Bayou where Cannon and several other oystermen were tonging for oysters. Big John Cannon was told he was under arrest for taking oysters off a leased bed without a permit. Not liking it one bit, Big John agreed to go with them if they would let him take his boy home first. At his dock, young Junie and the oysters were unloaded, then trying to stall the officers a little longer, Big John asked if he could change his wet clothes. Apparently having had enough of the perceived delay tactics, Moses Dykes figured he needed to let Big John Cannon know who was in charge. He drew his 38 pistol and fired a shot through the top of Cannon's Stetson hat. Unfortunately for Dykes, Cannon grabbed up his 12 gage shotgun from his boat and returned fire pointblank. He hit Dykes square in the chest, mortally wounding him. Gilbert told Cannon he wanted no more trouble from Cannon and drug his wounded partner away to seek medical help.

John Cannon, the independent fisherman was now a wanted man. There were two different accounts of his capture. A $250 bounty had been put on his head, so he went into hiding, spending the night on a log raft anchored in his beloved North Bay.

One version says that the next morning when Cannon was told that Moses John Dykes had died from his wounds, he turned himself in to the Sheriff of Bay County. The other, related in an article of the *Panama City Pilot* says that Cannon was able to elude capture until February 14, 1915 by hiding in the swamps of Little Goose Bayou. He was only caught after two bounty hunters discovered him. As the article reports, the bounty hunters noticed a dinner bucket hanging on a tree in the swamp and hid out in wait for someone to pick it up. When Cannon showed up carrying his shotgun, they confronted him and he gave up, feeling it better to be in custody of the Sheriff than living in the swamps with a bounty on his head.

Cannon was put on display down on Harrison Avenue in Panama City in the "Lions Pen" a steel cage on wheels that was used as the counties first jail. Several months in the small cramped quarters were later said to have had a life-long effect on Cannon.

The fishing community was solidly behind Cannon. Here was a man defending himself and exercising his God given rights to fish, who had been roughed up by the law. On the other hand, Commissioner Hodges was furious that such an atrocity had occurred, taking the life of one of his officers. The powers to be had decided to rethink their efforts and suspended all the North Bay leases. The battle that had begun with the passing of the shellfish laws was now joined. Would the courts up-hold the sanctity of an officers' life, killed in the line of duty, or would it side with the rights of the fishermen to pursue their trade?

On a Friday morning, in the latter weeks of November, the trial of Big John Cannon was finally begun. In a courtroom packed with fishermen, Judge D.K. Middleton, the defense attorney stated his case. He told the jurors that while it was unfortunate Moses John Dykes had been killed; his client could not be held responsible. He argued that Dykes, in the employ of the Shellfish Commission, was not really a law enforcement officer and did not have a warrant. He further stated that Cannon had a right to resist an illegal arrest and did not have to accompany the two men. Middleton chose to ignore that the law passed in the 1913 legislature specifically stated that "The Shellfish Commissioner and his deputies are hereby constituted police officers, with the power to arrest on view, without warrant, anyone violating the provisions of this act."

The prosecution team, headed by Ira Hutchinson and a member of the Dykes family argued that no one had the right to gun down an officer of the law. It came out in the trial that Dykes had actually fired two shots at Cannon before he opened fire with his shotgun. One can only surmise that when Dykes realized the gravity of Cannons movements to arm himself, he tried to defend his own life, but to no avail. He died on the banks of the North Bay doing the job he had been sworn to uphold, just like the countless other law enforcement officers who have taken the oath to serve and protect since that day.

The jury was sent to their deliberations that night, and after spending the early morning hours reviewing the testimony presented, they notified the bailiff they had reached a verdict.

On Saturday morning November 25, 1915 the court room filled with spectators, hushed as the jury entered the room. The judge asked them if they had a verdict, to which their foreman nodded affirmation.

The note was passed to the bench and the judge told Big John Cannon to stand and receive his verdict. In a booming voice he declared "Not Guilty!" The prosecution slumped in their chairs, the defense broke into smiles, and Big John Cannon cried like a baby.
Cannon would go back to fishing, but the burden of killing another man, whether justified or not, haunted

him for the rest of his life. His health had been broken by the year-long stay in the Lion's Pen and he suffered from arthritis the rest of his life.

In the last year before he died, his nephew Lincoln Ford Cavanaugh, would come and sit with him at a shack at Spanish Annie's in Panama City while his father and the Cannon boys went fishing. Cavanaugh related that his uncle would lie in bed and weep every night. Cavanaugh, who said he was "alive for the Lord" at the time, told his uncle about a Seventh Day Adventist preacher, W.W. Walker, who was preaching the gospel in town. Big John told him he would like to have the preacher come visit him. Cavanaugh notified the preacher and he came to visit, staying an hour with Big John. After that day Cavanaugh said he never heard his uncle weeping at night again. Even though Cannon never made a profession of faith, the preacher must have helped him reconcile with his misdeeds in life.

Big John Cannon died August 28, 1938 and was buried in the Old Southport Cemetery. In the author's interview with Ford Cavanaugh he stated that his family never spoke of the killing of Deputy Dykes. It was only many years later when fishing with Junie Cannon that Junie related to him what had happened that day. By the 1920's the once plentiful oyster beds of North Bay declined, either through over-fishing or neglect, and were never again able to produce enough to support the type of industry it had in earlier years. This resulted in a windfall for the Apalachicola Bay fishers who would begin dominating the markets of the panhandle with their products.

Commissioner Hodges could not believe that someone could get away with killing one of his men. Threats against Hodge's life and vows to destroy his vessel the "*Roamer*" became so frequent that Hodges had the U.S. government mount two one-pound cannons on the boat. Hodges argued that the guns were placed on the vessel to scare the fishermen into compliance. Although the cannons were never fired, the fishermen took it as a slap in the face that the state would send an armed vessel out to patrol their actions.

The "Roamer"

In a public report on the activities of the Shellfish Commission published in the *Florida Times-Union* he struck out at his distracters. He wrote;" It has been charged that the state is maintaining a gunboat to shoot down the fishermen of the state.... on account of so many threats being made against my life and to destroy the "*Roamer*", it was thought best to arm her with two one-pounder's, which were mounted on her by the United States government. They have never been used to fire upon anyone, and the only person killed was one of my deputies who was shot down in cold blood in broad daylight by a fisherman after having been arrested for a violation of the law. The murderer was set free without even a plea of insanity. I am practically the Sheriff for the entire state of Florida, who is expected to enforce the fish and oyster laws over a territory of over three thousand miles. It would be foolish to expect me to perform my duties unarmed."

Regardless of the feelings about him, Hodges saw to the business of the industry, replanting oyster beds around the state, promoting the emergence of a new shrimp industry in Florida and supporting the future conservation of the fisheries through strict law enforcement. However, he continued to note the lack of appreciation for the enforcement of the laws by the public.

The complaints and the hostility toward Commissioner Hodges fell on the ears of 1916 gubernatorial candidate Sidney Catts, a Baptist minister from Alabama. Catts took his campaign to the largely ignored voters in the west coast fish camps where he daily heard complaints about Shell Fish Commissioner Hodges arbitrary and dictatorial manner. The fishermen complained about the expensive methods Hodges used in enforcing the conservation laws and he made it a key point of his campaign. He maintained if he had been Governor, he would have vetoed the legislature's appropriation for the "*Roamer*." He also pledged "Not only will I remove Hodges when I get to be Governor, but I will sweep the "*Roamer*" off the seas." He vowed to sell the "*Roamer*" stating that "I am against the gunboat over our fishermen." He promised the fishermen he would allow them to pursue their occupation without interference from Tallahassee. In the highly controversial election of 1916 Catts defeated the favored candidate state comptroller W.V. Knott.

5

The One-Eyed Preacher Who Became Governor

Florida's gubernatorial election of 1916 was one that was unprecedented in the history of Florida politics. The State Democratic Party favorite and current state Comptroller William Knott was considered a "shoo in" to the governor's office. Knott was a fiscal conservative running on a platform of dealing with Florida's bank failures and the draining of the Everglades to create more land. His opponent was an unknown political newcomer named Sidney J. Catts.

Catts had become enamored with the idea of running for governor while attending a state Baptist convention in Tallahassee in 1914. Due to lack of hotel accommodations, he was a guest of Governor Park Trammell who told him the mansion was provided to the governor rent free. To the one-eyed Baptist minister struggling to feed a family of nine, it was a deal too good to be true. He threw his hat in the ring and ran as a populist, making his campaign theme one to "Win the little people." Catts platform was one of anti-Catholicism, statewide prohibition and support of the disenfranchised "little man."

Initially Catts was given little chance to win, but in the final analysis, it was his issues, not old time party politics that decided the outcome. The election of 1916 would see many firsts, and its result would shake the foundations of Florida politics.

Sidney Johnson Catts was named after Civil War General Albert Sidney Johnson. He grew up in rural Alabama and later attended Cumberland Law School in Tennessee. After graduation, he practiced law in Birmingham Al, but in early 1886 he became a devout Christian and decided to leave his law practice to be a full time preacher. Catts never attended a theological seminary, but he was a compelling, natural born orator and preacher who was adept at appealing to people's emotions. He was soon called as a pastor to churches in Fort Deposit, and later Tuskegee, Al. It was as a pastor that Catts first entered the political arena when he supported the prohibition efforts of the Southern Baptist church.

The 1890s saw many Southern Baptist Churches championing social issues in an attempt to shape politics. *The Alabama Baptist,* a newspaper of the church, regularly spoke out against alcohol, gambling, prostitution and Catholicism while embracing the plight of the small farmers. It was from these issues that one can trace Catts roots to the ideas that influenced his gubernatorial campaign in Florida in 1916.

Catts first attempt to enter politics as a candidate came in 1904 when he ran for congress, and though he did not win, he learned a political lesson that would shape his future campaigning style. Catts ran against a well-liked party insider of Alabama politics, J. Thomas Heflin. Taking the moral high road, Catts ran a campaign based on honesty and integrity, keeping to the election issues, not attacking his opponent and making few promises. Unfortunately, his ideas did not speak to the voters and Heflin was elected. In defeat, Catts took away from his campaign the knowledge that to get enough votes to defeat a political party insider, you have to get personal and speak of issues that stirred up the voters.

Disheartened, Catts continued in his ministry, but he had been bitten by the political bug, something that would drive him for the rest of his life. In 1911 he received a call to pastor a small Baptist church in Defuniak Springs, Fl. Catts served there until his resignation in 1914.

Upon leaving the ministry, Catts started a job as an insurance salesman for the Fraternal Insurance Company, which he later said was a way to make a living "while I ran for the governorship." His new job took him to the rural areas and coastal fishing villages of Florida where he made contact with the "little people" of Florida. The relationships he built along the way would help him when he ran against the entrenched political machine of Florida's Democratic Party in 1916. Although the Democratic Party in Florida was not totally aware or concerned with Sidney J. Catts at the time, they would soon be introduced to his populist campaign style.

The Democratic Party had ruled Florida politics since the end of the 1870s and to win the Democratic primary meant that the candidate would assume whatever office he had sought after the general election. Such was the expectation when the gubernatorial primary of 1916 began. Five individuals entered the race; William V. Knott, former state Treasurer and current state Comptroller who was considered the favorite, Ion L. Farris, attorney, two-time speaker of the House and current state senator, Fredrick M. Hudson, lawyer, counsel for the Florida Railroad Commission, former Senate President Frank A. Wood, a prominent banker and former House member from Miami, and Sidney J. Catts.

While Catts opponents all had political stature and backing, Catts took the route of involving the disenfranchised "little people" of the rural areas in his campaign. Tying a loudspeaker to his Model T Ford and driving from town to town, Catts was the first candidate to use an automobile in a statewide campaign. He went to the rural fishing villages and small towns where the majority of Florida's population lived; there he talked the politics of emotion, appealing to their fears, anger, and concerns. Building on their frustrations with government, Catts drove home his points against the Catholic menace to government, for statewide prohibition, and against state Shellfish Commissioner T.R. Hodges policies.

Catts championed the Anti-Catholic sentiment he had sensed in the rural communities. Since the early 1900s there had been a growing resentment and fear of Catholic influence and control in government.

This fear was nurtured by such people as Tom Watson from Georgia who published a newspaper called the *Jeffersonian*. In one series called "*The Roman*

Catholic Hierarchy," Watson warned that Catholic officeholders would be under the guidance of the church rather than the government. The *Jeffersonian* had a wide readership and influence in Florida's 1916 election. Other organizations supporting such anti-Catholic theories were soon formed and one that saw growth in Florida, the *Guardians of Liberty*, counted Catts as a member.

The organizations main purpose was to defeat any Catholic candidate for office. They were a semi-secret organization along the lines of the Masonic Lodges and published a weekly called the *Menace* in which they warned of Catholic inroads into American institutions. Catts rallied his supporters against the Catholic's through the pulpit, Sunday school classes and stump speeches. Catts told audiences that the Knights of Columbus in Tampa were storing ammunition for a "Negro revolution." Calling for support of the American flag and the little red school house against the Catholic convents and parochial schools, Catts tapped into the militant Protestantism and Florida nativism that also saw the rise of the Ku Klux Klan.

According to former Governor Fuller Warren in his book *How to Win in Politics*, "Catts hanged the Pope from every oak tree in West Florida during the years between 1910 and 1925." While his opponents were also Protestants, none but Catts took up the fight against the Catholics. By his taking on the mantel of the 'little man" in the fight against Catholicism, Catts had an issue that gave him their backing while taking the well-established Democratic Party by surprise.

This was the first time in Florida politics that religion had been put forward as a major campaign issue. In June of 1916, the Florida Democratic Party unknowingly played into Catts hands when they passed a controversial resolution at a meeting of their executive committee in Jacksonville, Florida.

Called the "Sturkie Amendment" after R.B. Sturkie, Chairman of the Resolutions Committee, it had five sections. First, to be considered a legal member and voter of the Democratic Party one had to be a white male. Second he must believe in the principals of the Democratic Party. Third, he should intend to support and vote for the candidates nominated by the Democratic Party. Fourth, that his voting will not be influenced in voting for or against any candidate by any religious test or on account of belief, denomination or sect with which the candidate is affiliated. And fifth, that he is not a member of any secret organization that attempts to influence political action or results. In their attempt to dampen the religious fervor raised by Catts, the Sturkie Amendment only threw fuel on the fire. Catts thought the amendment would force his withdrawal from the race but his campaign manager, J.V. Burke who was also a supporter of the *Guardians of Liberty*, told Catts not to worry; he would make the resolution unpopular.

The reaction, especially to sections four and five, was fast and loud. One writer to the *Bartow Courier-Informant* said, "If this plan to Romanize Florida inaugurated by the state democratic committee succeeds then the Roman hierarchy will control the names on the ballot…voters of Florida, are you willing to stand for this?" County democratic committees also adopted resolutions opposing sections four and five of the amendment.

In response to the outcry, the executive committee met again in Jacksonville on February 24, 1916 and repealed the controversial sections. Even though the resolution was amended, the damage to the Democratic Party had been done and Catts was the one who could tell the voters "I told you so." It would no longer be hard for him to convince voters that the Catholic Church was trying to control their public institutions and funds for their own purposes.

Having stirred up his supporters against Catholic intrusion in government, Catts promoted another hot topic of the times, prohibition.

In 1910 Florida voters had rejected a state amendment to their constitution calling for prohibition. Catts saw the issue as one he could easily embrace based on his Baptist faith as well as the knowledge that interjection of such an issue would distinguish him from his rivals. The prohibition movement in Florida had seen growth before the civil war but had waned afterwards. By 1904 the call for prohibition was not to just limit alcohol but to control what middle-class whites viewed as unruly black and lower working class whites. By 1904 twenty-seven of forty-six Florida counties were "dry" having exercised local option referendums to decide whether their county should be "wet" allowing alcohol sales or "dry" to prohibit such sales. The dry counties were made up of mostly sparsely populated areas while larger counties/cities remained wet. Franklin County, the only holdout in Middle Florida finally joined the dry column in 1915 leaving only six wet counties in the state; Escambia, Duval, St. Johns, Hillsborough, Monroe, and Palm Beach. With growing support for prohibition, no candidate came out in support of Franklin Counties decision and Catts saw it as the perfect vehicle for his campaign.

Catts then defended another "little man" issue, the government intrusion into the commercial fishermen's lives by the office of the State Shellfish Commission and its Commissioner T. R. Hodges.

The 1913 legislature had passed a comprehensive shellfish law that established the Commission and gave it broad police powers. Among other requirements fees were levied on retail and wholesale dealers, and fishermen had to pay fees for their fishing boats which in turn were used to finance the Commissioner and the department. The commercial fishing industry was not accustomed to such regulations, as heretofore commercial fishing had been considered a pastime and was not regulated. Many fishermen challenged the states authority and in 1915 an armed confrontation between Shellfish Commission Officer Moses Dykes and Southport, Florida commercial fisherman "Big John" Cannon resulted in Dykes murder. Hodges reaction to this incident was to arm the patrol vessel he used as a floating office *The Roamer* with two one-pound cannons, an action that infuriated the fishermen.

Catt's seized upon the fishermen's displeasure. Calling him "Commodore" Hodges, Catts identified with the fishermen who saw Hodges as a tyrannical and uppish, noting that he lived expensively and was far removed from their concerns. Catts pledged "Not only will I remove Hodges when I get to be governor, but I will sweep the "*Roamer*" off the seas."

The 1916 campaign for governor had begun with W.V. Knott and F.M. Hudson being seen as the main contenders, while Catts candidacy, which had concentrated on the rural areas, was given little chance. But a recent change in the election laws, called the Bryan primary law of 1913, would inadvertently play a major part in the election. The law, created to eliminate run-off primaries saw its first test in the 1916 Democratic primary. To avoid run-offs, the law called for voters to list their first and second place choices with the winner being the one who received the most of the two choices combined. When voters went to the polls on June 2, 1916 there was much confusion and error in tallying the results with it taking a week to determine the winner. When all counties were finally reported, much to everyone's surprise, Catts was declared the winner with 33,893 votes to Knott's 33,439.

Democratic Party members called on Knott to challenge the results but many state newspapers called on the Party to back the nominee. In a series of editorials, the *Tampa Morning Tribune* said that Catts, a virtual unknown, had defeated four of the party faithful while fighting opposition from the liquor industry, the state Democratic Party, the Catholic

Church and the state press. They went further to say the Party should accept Catts as their nominee while denouncing any attempt by Knott to challenge the results or run as an independent candidate. Knott supporters, seeking to overturn the election, seized upon the issue of Catts residency saying he had not lived in the state for the required five years to be eligible for office. The issue was nullified when it was found the five-year time period was from entry into the state until the date of election, by which Catts had qualified with four months to spare.

Knott decided to challenge the results in court and recounts were ordered with the issue finally ending up in Florida's Supreme Court. The court ordered the canvassing board to meet again and count the amended results and declare a winner. The canvassing board met on September 21, 1916 and five months after the primary, declared Knott the winner and gubernatorial nominee for the Democratic Party. Catts supporters cried foul, but Catts had a problem, how to get his name on the general election ballot. He could try to run as a progressive democrat on the democratic ticket, petition for his name to be added as an independent, or find another party affiliation to run under. The state Prohibition Party came to his rescue and agreed to nominate him as their party candidate.

Many of Catts supporters as well as others claimed the Democratic Party nomination had been stolen. Newspapers tended to back Catts claim to the nomination, while the *Miami Metropolis* printed an article titled "The Rape of a Governorship" that said the court had nominated Knott.

With a shortened election period for Knott, who had waited for the courts results before beginning campaigning, Catts had the upper hand with the voters and also had the benefit of more newspaper coverage than before the primary. Knott inadvertently gave Catts a propaganda plum when he accepted an offer from Shellfish Commissioner Hodges to spend the night and then travel to Tampa on the *Roamer* one evening after missing a train connection to his next stop. Knott's blunder all but assured the fishermen's vote for Catts. Catts supporters continued to tie Knott to the Catholic Church though he, like Catts, was a Baptist. One supporter went so far as to say Knott was "*the nominee of the four R's: rum, Romanism, railroads and red lights.*" In truth, both candidates supported prohibition, Catts was for a statewide ban on alcohol while Knott's supported the current local option allowing counties to vote their preferences.

The way Knott's had secured the nomination was a central point of the campaign and Catts played it for all it was worth. In stump speeches throughout the state he spoke about how the election had been stolen by the courts, referring to the Justices as "*five little tin gods*" and favoring their recall.

When a Pensacola newspaper editor was arrested and jailed for publishing an article accusing the court of misdeeds in the election, Catts further dared the court to put him in jail for contempt saying the people would tear down the building if the court did such a thing. One of Catts campaign managers came up with a phrase that resounded all over the state and the south: *"The Florida crackers have only three friends: God Almighty, Sears Roebuck, and Sidney J. Catts!"*

By the time of the election, public sentiment had turned to Catts, and based on the support he had contending the nomination had been stolen, it was obvious he would win. November 4, 1916 saw Florida voters go to the polls in overwhelming numbers for Catts. The final tally showed Catts with an almost 10,000 vote margin of 39, 546 votes to Knott's 30, 343.

Sidney J. Catts was sworn in as Florida's twenty-second Governor on January 2, 1917. He rode his Model T Ford in the inaugural parade with a banner attached that said *"This is the Ford that Got me there"*. In keeping with Catts style, he was the first governor ever sworn in carrying a loaded pistol in his pocket as protection against assassination threats. Catts achieved yet another first when his inauguration was filmed with a motion picture camera.

True to his word to the fishermen, one of the first things Catts did in office was to fire "Commodore" Hodges and order the sale of the *Roamer* through the legislature.

Running as a candidate of the "little man", Sidney J. Catts had defied all the naysayers and odds. He had built his campaign on the social issues of religion, prohibition, and less government control and had prevailed. By inflaming the rural populations to rise up against the state Democratic Party machine they had flexed their political muscle and elected an unknown with no political experience as Governor.

Florida's most controversial election had ended filled with many unprecedented firsts. He was the first candidate for statewide election to ever campaign using an automobile. Never before had anyone gone up against the state political machine in a one party state and succeeded. For the first time in Florida politics, the state Supreme Court had been involved in determining the winner of an election. After losing in the primary that used a new, confusing system to determine the winner, he was the first to run as a candidate for another party and win the gubernatorial election. Catts was also the first of only two Prohibition Party candidates to ever even win an election in the United States.

By running as a populist and campaigning solely on social issues, Sidney J. Catts had turned Florida's old time party politics on its ear and won the election of 1916.

Inaugural parade for Governor Sidney Johnston Catts - Tallahassee, Florida from Florida Archives

6

Tungston Plantation

Car loads of people driving on highway 27 outside of Monticello frequently pass by a piece of lost Florida history-the Tung oil groves of Capps, Florida. There was a time not too long ago when the roads of Jefferson County were adorned by blooming Tung trees. Every spring their dark green, heart-shaped leaves would reveal their beautiful whitish, rose colored flowers that produced tung nuts. No matter its beauty, the fact is that *all* parts of the Tung tree are poisonous, especially the nut. A native tree of China for 40 centuries, Tung has been grown commercially in warmer climates of the United States for the oil that is extracted from its seed, or nut. One Tung tree alone will produce two tons of nuts equaling 100 gallons of Tung oil annually through its thirty-year life-span. Tung oil hardens when exposed to air resulting in a transparent, plastic-like coating. Tung oil was used in varnish, linoleum, printer's ink and for coating the insides of cans and insulating electrical circuits, it was once considered the very best oil for high quality, quick-drying paint.

Introduced into the Gulf region of the United States in the 1900s and Jefferson County in 1906, Tung oil production quickly became a major industry by the 1930s. When Chinese imports were stopped because of World War II, the national production of Tung oil was declared strategic to our countries defense. This was due to its uses in preventing rust and reducing friction on engine parts. By the late-1950s, there were over 12,000 acres of Tung trees planted in Jefferson County. Tung mills were in the southeast edge of Monticello at Jumpy Run, Tungston at Capps, General Tung at Lamont, and Leon Tung in Tallahassee. Other production areas were centered around Gainesville and Marianna, Fla., Bogaloosa, La., and Poplarville, Miss. One of the largest operations producing Tung oil was once located outside of Monticello, Florida near the intersection of U.S Route 19 & 27.

This unincorporated area of Jefferson county was called Capps and its major claim to fame was Tungston Plantation. The plantation was owned by Everett P. Larsh, an industrialist from Ohio, and managed by L. H. Crampton. During the 1940s and 50s it was the largest Tung operation in the U.S. under single ownership. The plantation designated 8,000 of its 16,000 acres to Tung trees. Ripened Tung nuts were harvested and processed in the mill at Capps.

The Tung Oil Plant on the Tungston Plantation Archives of Florida/Stokes

Domestic production peaked in the late 1950s but soon began to decline. Foreign competition and cheaper oilseeds like linseed, soybean, canola, and the development of synthetic oils plus shifting parity prices led many growers to seek other crops. Hard winter freezes in the 50s and 60s devastated many commercial orchards. The destruction caused by Hurricanes Betsy and Camille in 1965 and 1969 were the final nails in the coffin for the domestic industry. Today, all the Tung orchards in the area have been abandoned, most of the trees bulldozed and the land used for home sites, pasture, or timber.

**Abandoned Tungston mill building
photo by Mike Woodfin**

Today the old buildings of Tungston have long been demolished and a few Tung trees stand as lonely witnesses of their past glory.

7

Sulphur Spring in North Florida

Tourism was slow coming to Florida, with the first tourists showing up in the mid-nineteenth century. Early tourism in Florida was first confined to those of more affluent means seeking a warmer climate to address medical ailments such as rheumatism, consumption or other infirmities through hydrotherapy in Sulphur springs. Others came to escape the harsh northern winters, or to hunt, fish, swim, or view wildlife in its woods and waters. Traveling first by rail to Georgia, then steamer into Florida they found a warmer climate, but harsh living conditions.

St. Augustine was one of the first cities to see an influx of visitors, among them railroad magnate Henry Flagler who brought his ailing wife. Disgusted with the local accommodations he decided to build his own. His legacy as a developer and promoter of Florida was instrumental to the growth of tourism on Florida's east coast. Henry Plant, another railroad magnate was instrumental for the development of Florida's west coast. Other's seeking the healing mineral waters of Florida encouraged the expansion of health spa's to the northern parts of Florida. Resorts sprang up around the natural springs in White Springs, Hampton Springs, Newport and Panacea. It was widely believed that soaking oneself in the mineral waters or even drinking the water eliminated toxins in the body and increased the blood flow. A higher blood flow increased the body temperature's that then killed harmful germs and viruses. By soaking in the springs the infirmed were promised not only the healing of a multitude of infirmities, but reduced stress and better skin condition. Sulphur springs, caused by the release of Sulphur dioxide gas escaping into the air were prevalent in northern Florida and entrepreneurs were quick to capitalize on their healthful benefits. One of the longest running resorts was the Hampton Springs Hotel in Perry, Fl.

8

The Hampton Springs Hotel

State of Florida/Archives

The Hampton Springs Hotel once known as "Dixie's Famous Spa" was located four miles west of Perry, Florida off county road 356. In its heyday it was a destination for invalids and the idle rich seeking health and relaxation in the warm waters of a natural Florida spring. There are two stories concerning how the springs became known, one true and the other the result of early Florida tourist promotion. First the promotional story.

Legend had it that early Taylor County resident Joe Hamilton discovered the springs after being told of its healing powers by an old Indian. His wife who had suffered for years from rheumatism was instantly relieved of her pains once she bathed in the springs. Hamilton then rushed to purchase the land around the springs and received it by way of a $10.00 government grant. His heirs then built a hotel there in 1904. In truth, 40 acres of land around a spring which fed into the Fenholloway River, known as Rocky Creek Mineral Springs, was purchased in 1879 from a Madison County couple by Benjamin W. And Joseph L. Hampton. The land then sat dormant for years.

In 1908 the Hampton families, to turn a profit off the investment, formed the Hampton Springs Hotel and Mineral Company and built a two-story 70 room hotel around the springs. The hotel was moderately successful when South Georgia Railway tycoon, J.W. Ogelsby of Adel, Ga decided to invest in the property. The hotel was expanded in 1915 and boasted its own power and water plant which supplied steam heat, bath pools, warm Sulphur baths in tubs or showers, and elaborate fountains. All food served in the hotel came from a garden and farm on the grounds. The natural spring water was channeled into a covered indoors swimming pool then back out to the springs. Ogelsby extended his railway to Perry allowing easier access to the resort and began advertising its luxury accommodations. With his promotional efforts, his fortunes soon started to rise. Olgesby brought passenger trains to his resort, and even had a special parlor car outfitted and named the *Hampton Springs* of which he charged passengers an exorbitant fee to ride. By 1927 Ogelsby lost interest in running his hotel and decided to lease the property to Chicago developer Arnold Joern's in a 99-year lease.

Joern's, seeing the potential of the property formed an exclusive membership only spa called the Hampton Springs Club and billed itself as *"Florida's most beautiful year round retreat."* Joern's founded the Hampton Springs Properties, Inc. with himself as president, Charles E. Hesson as vice president and manager, and Sam Turnes as secretary and treasurer. Their executive offices were in the Wrigley Building in Chicago, Il.

The hotel was expanded and the grounds surrounding the hotel soon boasted its own railroad depot, a nine-hole golf course which could also be utilized as an "aviation landing field", tennis courts, stables with miles of riding trails, and an outdoor dance pavilion. Inside the hotel was a gambling casino and a grand ballroom. Wicker chairs adorned the verandas overlooking lush gardens and planters. The club leased land on Spring Creek six miles away where they had a private hunting and fishing lodge. Visitors were invited to hunt quail, deer, wild turkey, ducks and geese, all found "in great numbers."

"Inviting to men, women and children of refinement" the rates varied from $4.00 to $7.50 a day which included room and meals. Special weekly and monthly as well as family rates were offered. A private covered launch was employed to take guests on a 12-mile excursion down the Fenholloway River to the Gulf. Guests were invited to become members of the Hampton Springs Club (by invitation only) and enjoy reduced rates on hotel services as well as participating in hotel and water sales profits.

The Hotel created a land boom around the area with some landowners pricing their lands more than one million dollars. Calling itself the *"National Health Resort"*, the luxury hotel promoted its Hampton Springs water as the cure for "rheumatism, indigestion, dyspepsia, stomach, kidney, and bladder troubles, as well as gastritis and skin diseases." A private bottling plant on the grounds shipped Hampton Springs water through mail order nationwide. One could buy a case of 12 half-gallon bottles for six dollars or a five-gallon demijohn (bulbous narrow-necked bottles) for four dollars. Rebates of $1.00 were offered for customers returning empty bottles.

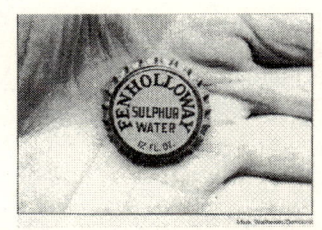

Bottle-top from Hampton Springs Water Bottle

A promotional brochure of Taylor County circa 1923 featured an image of the Hampton Springs Hotel with the heading OUR INVITATION. The text reads:

"Anyone interested is invited to come to Taylor county. The home seeker, the tourist, and the sportsman are all welcome. Perry is known as a *Glad Hand Town*, where the visitor is given a cordial greeting, and made to feel at home. If you are interested in fruit growing, trucking, farming, dairying, raising livestock or poultry, if you are interested in hunting or fishing, or just wish to rest and recuperate, you are asked to come and investigate opportunities. Meet our people, see our proved and unimproved lands, learn of the great variety and yield of the crops, partake of the pleasures our section has to offer, then if you are pleased, make your plans to stay with us."

The owners of the hotel saw their fortunes change in the thirties when automobile traffic began to allow tourists to travel without dependence on the railways. The lure of Florida's Sulphur springs also was beginning to decline as its medicinal properties began to be questioned. To maintain their business, the hotel leased itself out in the mid-thirties and forties to the military for use as barracks for airmen testing airplanes at the Perry-Foley airport. After the war it continued in business as an exclusive hunting and fishing resort. A fire destroyed the Hotel in 1954.

9

The Wakulla Beach Hotel

If you want to take a trip back in Florida history, turn left onto Wakulla Beach road off highway 98 just a few miles west of St Marks. The two-mile drive through the cabbage palms and hardwoods will slowly pull you back to a simpler time. The road, formerly known as Hotel Avenue, dead-ends at the gulf, more appropriately at Apalachee Bay. To your right lay the ruins of the Walker Hotel, one of three built through the years.

It all started as a dream of Daisy Walker, a state Senators wife who wanted to create a town called East Goose Creek. Her first attempt was to build a hotel on their beach property. She opened the first hotel in 1915 and business prospered but she decided in 1920 to convert the hotel to her residence and built a second hotel closer to the beach.

As anyone who lives near the beach knows, you are at the mercy of the changing weather of wind, waves, and tides when living at the coast. In 1928, the winds won out when a hurricane destroyed the hotel. Not to be discouraged, Daisy rebuilt the hotel, this time a two story affair with kitchen and dining rooms on the first floor and guest rooms on the second. Calling their location "Walkers Point" it was soon filled with year-round guests. Daisy finally had her hotel, but the town was never to be. Daisy died in 1935 and her husband deeded the land to the U.S. Fish and Wildlife Service in 1949 to become a part of the St. Marks National Wildlife Refuge.

Remains of Daisy Walker's Wakulla Beach Hotel 1955
State of Florida/Archives

10

Wakulla County Seine Yards

The Walkers Hotel at East Goose Creek was well known as a tourist location early in the twentieth century but it was West Goose Creek that drew the fishermen. The West Goose Creek Seine yard, one of sixteen seine yards located between St. Marks and Turkey Point in Franklin County is one of the area's oldest and longest surviving seine yards. Along with West Goose Creek, only two other locations survived into the modern times; Shell Point and Bottoms. It was at these seine yards where fishermen of old (and some still today) came to fish for mullet, Florida's "money fish." Many of the seine yards were either named after the landowner, the property itself, or the area in which it was located.

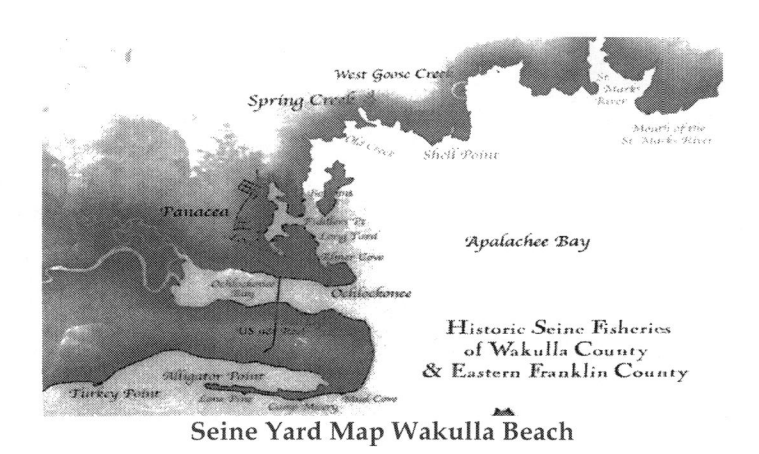

Seine Yard Map Wakulla Beach

The term seine yard applies to an obstacle free area of shallow water off a beach where a beach seine net could be set and then hauled out and the catch processed. A seine net is a wall of webbing supported by a cork line and weighted by a lead line. In the old days, it was constructed of heavy cotton twine of small mesh, so that the fish do not normally gill. A seine encloses fish and as the ends of the net are drawn together the catch becomes concentrated in an ever-decreasing area. Usually a 600 to 800-yard seine net would be set from a boat. One end would be anchored on the beach and the other rowed off shore in a semi-circular manner. As the fish would travel along the shoreline they would be enclosed in the net. Once encircled the boat would row back to shore and the net hauled in either by teams of horses or by many hands on shore.

In the "run season" lasting from October to December, mullet would naturally frequent these shallow water areas as they moved east to west along the coastline keeping their "right eye to the shore" as they moved from West Goose Creek around to Shell Point, Bottoms, Ochlockonee Bay and Turkey Point. In early Florida, after harvesting their fall crops, the Middle Florida plantation owners would load up their families in wagons and come to the seine yards to catch mullet. They would set up camps and spend their days catching and processing the mullet. The fish would be cleaned then processed by smoking or salting. The fish were then stored in wooden barrels for shipping or storage for later use. Many plantation owners used mullet as a source of food for their slaves. Others would come to barter farm goods in exchange for fish. All in all, it was a festive occasion.

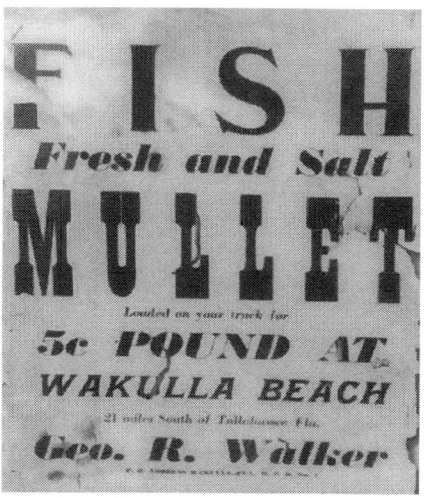

Advertisement Wakulla Beach

As advertised by the poster, fishermen at the Wakulla Beach seine yard operated a profitable business during the run season. George Walker, son of Daisy Walker even offered the extra service of loading it in your truck. Other seine yards in Dickerson Bay, Smith Creek, Ochlockonee Bay, Alligator Point and St. Teresa also profited from sales. Throughout the first half of the twentieth century the seine yards operated unabated. But new regulations passed in the second half of the century would be the cause of their extinction. From closed seasons, to gear regulations, to an all-out net ban, the seine yards suffered. Today they are but a memory passed down among fishing families of the "good old days."

11

Is a Mullet a Fish or a Bird?

Folks in Wakulla County take their fishing and hunting seriously. They like the freedom of going out on the bays or in the woods to put food on the table. They don't like to be hindered, and when they are, they fight back. In 1915 a new law established seasons for mullet fishing. It created a closed season that encompassed the normal fall October through December "run season" and created an open season in January and February. To the local mullet fishermen this was absurd. Pity the poor Shell Fish Commission Officer who in 1916 arrested a local fisherman charging him with fishing for mullet out of season. The fishery laws were new, having just been codified in 1913 and 1915. To the outdoors enthusiast who felt fishing was a "*God given right*," being told what he could and could not do was incomprehensible.

The fisherman decided to fight the case and it came before Wakulla County Judge R. Don McLeod. The defense introduced a biologist who testified that a mullet was not a fish because it had a gizzard. He further stated that since only birds have gizzards, the stripped mullet was in actuality a fowl i.e. a member of the poultry family. The man's lawyer then argued that since the mullet is a member of the poultry family and there is no closed season on poultry, he should be freed. Judge McLeod, after hearing both sides ruled in favor of the fisherman, acquitting him of all charges. McLeod would go on to sit on the bench for another nine years, retiring after a 28-year career as a jurist.

Judge R. Don McLeod

His famous ruling that a mullet is a bird because it has a gizzard occurred in the old Wakulla County courthouse. The old courthouse, built in 1894 from heart of pine lumber was the last wooden courthouse in Florida. Today a hand-carved mullet weathervane made of cypress is displayed over the restored courthouse building in homage to his famous ruling and to the fact that in Wakulla County…the Mullet is King. To prove this point, the annual "Mighty Mullet Maritime Festival Day" proclamation states;

Whereas, Wakulla County has a rich maritime heritage linked to mullet fishing dating from the early 1900s when men left home to work the nets in seine yards and wagonloads of produce from farms to the north arrived at such sites as Shell Point, Goose Creek, Bottoms Road, Dickerson Bay, Smith Creek, Ochlockonee Bay, Alligator Point and St. Teresa to barter for salted mullet; Whereas, the mullet windvane atop Wakulla County Courthouse reminds us of the legal battles waged in the name and pronouncement of one Judge that the mullet is actually a chicken rather than a fish because it has a gizzard."

Mullet weathervane atop Wakulla Courthouse

A little further south of Wakulla County in Hillsborough County, former Senator Pat Whitaker had fought the same battle. It was in 1919 when he, as a young lawyer, took on a case of six men arrested in Tampa Bay for fishing out of season. Whitaker did some research and found that the mullet had a gizzard, which since it is a bottom feeder, would help it digest the sand it picked up while feeding.

Years later when talking to Tampa Tribune writer Paul Wilder, Senator Whitaker told him; "When it came my time to talk I got up and told the judge that these men were charged with catching fish out of season and in fact all they caught were mullet," he said. "Then I dragged out the books showing that no fish has a gizzard but a mullet has." Whitaker went on to suggest that mullet might indeed be birds. "Whales live in the water but they aren't fish. Beavers live in the water and they aren't fish. I conceded that mullet lived in the water like a fish, but that didn't make him a fish," he later recalled. "The only thing I could think of was that these mullet were some kind of aquatic fowl."

The judge dismissed the case. To avoid any further such litigation, the Florida legislature rewrote its laws concerning mullet to specify that regardless of what it may be, it was regulated.

12

The Wakulla Swamp Volcano

People say there is no way a volcano could be in Florida. But early inhabitants as far back as the Indians swore there was one in Wakulla County. In the 1830s people would report seeing thick, black plumes of smoke mingled with white clouds of steam rising 25 miles southeast of Tallahassee. Standing atop the capitol or the courthouse copula in Tallahassee they would report seeing a red glare in the sky and black, white and grey smoke accompanied by loud denotations. Mariners used the smoke as a landmark to ports along the coast. Some said it was not in Wakulla County but in Jefferson County in Township 4 South-Range 3 East-04, (the Pinhook area of *Gum Swamp* area located inside the St. Marks Refuge.) Regardless, it was too obvious to ignore.

A Volcano in Florida?

There were many explanations…it was a burning pine tree struck by lightning, a signal light set by smugglers, pirates, or civil war deserters, a lightered log fire used in a "sugar furnace" boiling caldrons of grinded sugar cane juice, a hermit's campfire, ceremonial Indian fires, campfires of negro priests conducting voodoo orgies, a moonshine still, a confederate salt works (which Union boats reportedly shelled), or a large natural gas field under the Gulf of Mexico. Indian legend had it that the smoke was the result of a young Indian warrior tending a "home fire" to lead his Chieftain father back to his tribe. Sailors sighting the smoke would comment saying "The old man of the swamp is smoking his pipe today." Local Negros would say it was" the Devils tar kiln." Florida Crackers, taking a more nuanced view would say "it was a passel of lighter logs afire or a patch of mud that gets dry and burns." Whatever the cause, none could explain its longevity.

A Wakulla resident, Mr. Frank Duggle reported sighting the volcano's activity in June of 1880. He said that the light of the volcano and its "loud, rumbling" noise had frightened his family so much that they ran out of their house at midnight fearing another earthquake. Another writer to the *"Florida Dispatch"* in September 1883 reported seeing the smoke hundreds of times. He attempted to locate its source but could not navigate through the "jungles" of the Aucilla, Wacassia, Ecofina, Fenholloway and Pinhook Rivers where they intercept each other.

Reward offers were made by some New York newspapers to the first person to locate and solve the mystery of the smoke but none was ever collected.

In an 1890 article in his HANDBOOK OF FLORIDA, Charles Ledyard Norton wrote about the volcano;

To the southeast and south of Tallahassee there extends a vast belt of flat woods, merging into an almost impenetrable tangle of undergrowth and swamp. It is a famous hunting-ground, and somewhere within its shades is the alleged Wakulla volcano. The curious inquirer is sure to hear the most contradictory statements regarding this mystery. He will be told by some that it can be seen from any high observatory in the vicinity, and by others that it cannot be seen from any save those most southerly uplands. He will meet people who have seen the smoke almost every day of their lives, others who declare that there is no such and still others who say that they never heard of it. It seems to be pretty well established, however, that ever since the country was settled, and, according to Indian tradition, long prior to that, a column of smoke or vapor has been visible in favorable weather, rising from a fixed point far within the jungle, to which no man has yet been able to penetrate. Several expeditions have been organized to solve the mystery, but none of them have penetrated more than twelve or fifteen miles into the morass. Once or twice New York newspapers have sent representatives with orders to solve the problem, but, according to the local version, they have always proved recreant to their duty as soon as the difficulties in the way became apparent. The "volcano," therefore, bids fair to remain a mystery until some well-equipped expedition undertakes its discovery.

A column of smoke was pointed out to the author as the alleged "volcano," and on several successive days' bearings were taken with a pocket compass from the cupola of the Court-house at Tallahassee. The smoke in favorable weather was always visible in the same place, rolling up in strong volume, usually dense and dark like the smoke from a furnace chimney. the author was assured by a Northern gentleman, long resident in Tallahassee, that it was often lighted with a faint glow at night. It is believed by many to be vapor from a boiling spring. possibly intermingled with inflammable that occasionally ignites. In March,1891, the author, with J.B. Staley, of Tallahassee, as guide tried to reach the "volcano '' and nearly lost his life in the attempt. Later in the same season Messrs. Castleman and Barbour, with Staley as guide, Spent two weeks in the search, but with no better success. C. L. N.

Then in a July 17,1893 article the *Chicago Tribune* claimed to have finally discovered its source proclaiming:

Solution of The Wakulla Volcano- The Great Mystery of Florida Proves to Be Burning Earth

Sumterville (Fla) Times: "In the tangled woods of that part of the great Florida swamp that borders on the territory of phosphate mining a prospector has just made an interesting discovery. He has solved the famous mystery of the Wakulla Volcano. Instead of a volcano he has found a vast expanse of burning earth.

Learned men for a long time have held that an active volcano must exist in this hitherto inaccessible region. For many years' scientists, adventurers, and explorers have made spasmodic attempts to penetrate the swamp, lured on by the strange tales of simple people who live in its vicinity and by the wonderful phenomena which they themselves have observed from afar.
The unvarying report of the country folk has been that from this great swamp from the time of their fathers and grandfather's clouds of steam and smoke have risen in volumes, and that at certain periods flames of fire have been seen to belch forth as from the crater of a huge volcano, making at night a most weird display on the distant horizon. Indeed, since no one has seen the actual spot, and no adequate cause could be given of the strange phenomena, they have been regarded as a sort of superstition.

The swamp is located on the Gulf of Mexico and is many square miles in extent. It is just south of Tallahassee and covers a part of Wakulla and Jefferson Counties. It is most easily approached from the State of Georgia. During the Civil War union gunboats on the way to the siege of New Orleans anchored off the place and shelled the spot where the smoke was issuing in belief it was a camp of confederate soldiers engaged in refining salt.

Six or seven years ago a New York newspaper man offered a reward of $1,000 to the man who would penetrate the swamp, explain the mystery, and prepare a full account for his columns.

Since that time a continued interest has been manifested in the mystery. One adventurer, who has made his way within two miles of the supposed volcano, climbed to the top of a tall tree to catch a view of the distant wonder, but the boughs gave way beneath him and he nearly lost his life. Mr. W.A. Barber, who was formerly connected with the Florida geological survey made several excursions into the swamp. He carefully surveyed the region, and after making observations of the strange fire he located its situation, but without reaching the spot.

Mr. Martin, a prospector for a firm of Georgia capitalists who have extensive interests in mining Florida phosphate, is the man that made the conclusive discovery, largely to satisfy his own curiosity. He found the surface of the swamp honey-combed with holes made by the fire. They extended for miles and miles, showing that the fire had steadily burned for many years. The depth of the vast fissures, was about five feet, and in the bottom the deepest salt water was found, which proved the surface of the swamp was but little higher than the level of the gulf, and underground channels were discovered which drain the swamp of its waters.

As he approached the locality where the fire was active the air was filled with thick smoke, the stench of decaying fish became almost unbearable, and the booming like that of a distant cannon was heard.

The earth of roots and coarse vegetable fibers protected by a waterproof moss, like an immense peat bog, has fed the fire with an endless supply of fuel. In such a soil the flame would smolder for months during the rainy season to burst forth when the sun and the drought returned. The tall trees, to the very top of which the flames climbed, account for the phenomena of the sprouting fires at which people have stood aghast for generations.

The success of the discovery is due to the fact that the approach was made from the north side, by which the pools and dense growth of canebreak, which have been hindrances to former explorers, were avoided. Plenty of time and abundance of provisions were available and the work of having a path through the dense undergrowth and fallen trees was taken up systematically and patiently.

It is impossible to estimate the time the Wakulla fire may have been burning, but to judge from the vast expanse already covered it must have been lighted at least a hundred years ago, and there is fuel in this deep morass to fuel it a thousand more."

The volcano seemed to disappear after an earthquake hit Charleston, South Carolina on August 31, 1886 with its tremors felt as far away as Florida. People surmised that if the smoking fissure had opened years ago, it now had been closed by the earthquakes effects. But the story persisted and people continued to report sightings of the smoke and search for its source.

Only four people have been known to find the volcano's source; Judge A.L. Porter of Crawfordville and Forester James Kirkland in the 1920s, and Fred Wimpee and William Wyatt in the 1930s.

Mr. William Wyatt spoke about the volcano in a speech given to the *Tallahassee Historical Society* April 11, 1935. He said he went into the swamp area during the dry season of 1932-33 to explore the area. He reported finding residual flint rock of the Miocene age that appeared to have been blown out of sinkholes whose edges were rounded as if they had been subjected to intense heat. While he would have liked to have said it was from a volcano, he had to take the geological nature of the area into account. Florida is home to many underground limestone formations full of cavities. He theorized the swamp deposited decaying trees and debris in these cavities, some very deep and, with the assistance of the springs, deposited the matter far away into its caverns. When at a later date the waters receded, the peat combusted and started burning and smoking. The fires continued, occasionally breaking through in weak parts of the earth and emitting the smoke seen from afar. It is his theory that they were extinguished with the Charleston earthquake. Mr. W.T. Cash, the Florida State Historian later agreed with his theory in a letter to then State Geologist Herman Gunter.

In a 1941 interview with Florida State College for Women student Bettye Burch, Wyatt reiterated his theory that the smoke came from a place that had been washed out by waves and heavy rains causing sinkholes with huge blank walls of stone. The holes then filled with debris and made peat, which burned for five to six hundred years. After an earthquake, the area settled to sea level and water pouring into the holes created a quasi-volcano. He further surmised that water has since covered the peat filled sinkholes putting out the fires. Historically the area has been in and out of the gulf at least five times and is now (in 1941) a marsh area. Wyatt said the area gets dark quickly and others are reluctant to go explore the area with him. "There are many superstitions about the smoking volcano," he said, "and it is hard to get a negro to go in with me. But I should like to investigate it again, because there is still much mystery to be involved."

It seems that all the accounts of those trying to figure out the mystery were hindered by access to the area, citing tangled vines and "jungle." This can be explained by the fact that it was not until 1954 that highway US 19, which cuts through the swamp area, was completed between Wakulla and Perry. It was also before extensive cypress logging had been done in the area. Prior to that time attempts to access the suspected location had to be made by boat or horseback, then by foot. The adventurer would have to be assisted by a team of men to cut their way through the swamp while fighting mosquitos, snakes and alligators.

After years of studying the accounts of the volcano Angus Laird of Tallahassee surmised there were two sites. One found by Porter and Kirkland and another by Wimpee and Wyatt. In constructing the highway to Perry in 1949 Huey D. Langdale of Newport found a location that matched Wyatt's description in the future road right of way. Unfortunately for historians, the road crew filled the hole in with 34 truckloads of rock and fill (about 14 to 20 tons a truckload.) Langdale noticed the unusual rock and kept some samples that he embedded into the front of his gas station in Newport, the only current proof of the volcano's existence today.

Civilization has made the trip today easier but that does not mean one can particularly find the site. In 2002 R.C. Balfour III, author of *"In Search of the Aucilla"* wrote of his attempt to find the volcano's source guided by Pete Gerrell. Afterwards, he provided directions and a map to show its approximate location. Judge Porter also provided a map and directions stating; "go to the Wakulla/Jefferson line, then go south two miles to a fence across St. Joe Paper Company land. A tree with slats mentioned by early volcano hunters stands south of the fence. The volcano site can be found 3/4s of a mile southeast deep in the swamp."

If you were to look on a USGS map of Jefferson County, its approximate location would be in Section 4S-3E-04 in the Pinhook Springs area. For those seeking adventure, I recommend you try to find it.

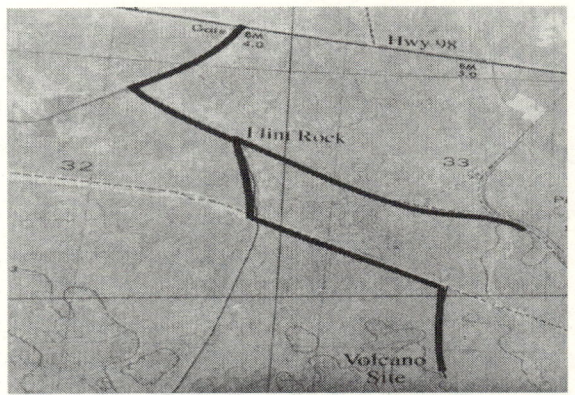

USGS map by R.C. Balfour in *"In Search of the Aucilla"*

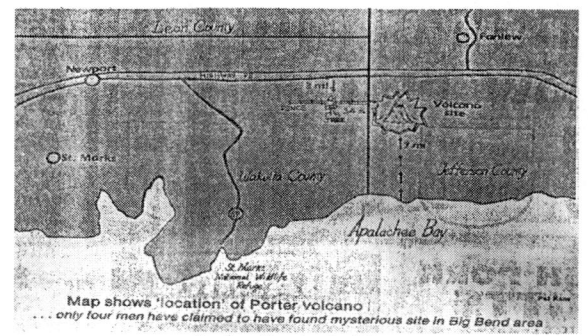

Map shows 'location' of Porter volcano
... only four men have claimed to have found mysterious site in Big Bend area

Judge Porter's Map

13

Confederate Salt Works

Caldron used to boil saltwater

Salt has long been a necessary commodity to man. The word salary is derived from the word salt. From the times of early civilizations man has used salt as currency and for trade. It uses have been around since before the beginning recordings of history. It is one of the most effective methods of food preservation known to man. Terms such as "not worth his salt" were used about trading slaves for salt in ancient Greece. The Bible refers to salt over 30 times. It was also thought that throwing salt on a coffin before burial would keep away the devil.

Because it is surrounded on three sides by salt water, salt has played a major role in Florida history. First as a preservative for fisheries products and later to supply a fledging confederate army.

During the Civil War, salt works dotted the Florida coast from Panama City to Tampa. St. Andrew Bay in Panama City and St. Joseph Bay in Port St. Joe were especially proficient sites due to the high salt content of their waters. It has been said that these salt works and their contribution to the Confederacy were a main reason it survived. Florida salt was used to preserve meat, tan hides, and dye uniforms. It was meat preserved from Florida cattle that made sure the troops had food to eat.

A salt work consisted of a large 60 to 100 gallon kettle like caldron or boiler that was placed on bricks under which a fire was set to boil out the water and leave the salt. The salt was then set out in large drying pans or boards then refined by repeated dipping, pouring and drying. Not only would the sun dry the salt, it would also bleach it white. Such was the need, the confederacy exempted salt makers from military service and many took them up on the offer, working night and day. But it was not necessarily a safe profession. The works were manned by confederates and their slaves. Many slaves would escape and later lead Union troops to the salt works locations.

In 1862, to establish a blockade of Florida ports, the Union created two commands, the South Atlantic and the East Gulf Blockading Squadrons. While charged with capturing blockade runners, they also began an assault on the salt works. Union gunboats patrolling the coast would shell any sites where they saw smoke arising from the marshes or detach troops to flush out the salt makers and destroy their furnaces.

Throughout the war thousands of salt works were located and destroyed. The buildings would be burned, furnaces smashed, the salt mixed with sand, and any equipment used destroyed. Salt workers would retreat at the sign of Union soldiers and wait until they were through destroying their works. They would then return, rebuild, and go back into operation.

Evidence of these salt works still exist along the Gulf coast. On Cape San Blas the Old Salt Works cabins on State road 30E are constructed on a Civil War salt works site.

To the careful observer surveying the coastline, one can see piles of elevated bricks or limestone rubble where the kettles sat. Usually they were in areas affected by a high tide that would wash in then leave pools of salt water that the workers would boil out the salt.

Remnants' of old salt works

14

Ed Ball and The Wakulla Springs Lodge

Wakulla Springs Lodge/ Florida Archives

Built in 1937 the Wakulla Springs Lodge stands as a memorial to a man, and a marker of a simpler yet elegant way of life. The man was Mr. Edward Gresham Ball whose favorite saying was "Confusion to the enemy!"

Ed Ball was a man to be reckoned with in Florida politics from the 1930s to the 70s. As the chief architect of the infamous "Pork Chop Gang," a group of 20 powerful North Florida legislators from the

1930s to 60s, he controlled the state. While Ball never held public office, he pulled the financial strings that made people dance. As trustee of his sister Jessie Ball DuPont's estate, he built it into a two-billion-dollar estate that included the Florida East Coast Railway, the St. Joe Paper Company, the Florida Sugar Company, The Nemuours Foundation, Box R Ranch, the Wakulla Springs Lodge, the holdings of the *Florida National Group* of 185 banks, numerous container plants in the U.S, England, and Ireland, and 1.2 million acres of land in Georgia and the Florida panhandle.

Ball purchased the land surrounding Wakulla Springs from George T. Christie in 1934. Christie had owned the springs from 1925 to 1934 and had promoted it as a tourist spot. He put in a 33 1/3-foot diving tower, a swimming pier and in 1931 introduced glass-bottomed boat tours.

Ball closed the springs to the public and built the Lodge as a guest house for entertaining his rich and powerful friends. It contained twenty-seven rooms featuring pecky cypress paneling, marble floors, hand- made ceramic tiles, wrought iron, and hand painted murals on the ceilings. Costing over $75,000 to build it was a 1930s marvel. To provide telephone service to his lodge he had the St. Joe Telephone Company run a line 89 miles to the site. Ball reopened the area with his lodge complete in 1937.

Ball always had an eye out to make a buck and in 1941 he hired Newton Perry as general manager of the springs. Perry who had previously worked at

Silver Springs, was an avid diver and swim instructor who saw promise in the clear waters of Wakulla Springs. He began promoting it as a filming location and lured MGM Studios to film two Tarzan movies at the site as well as Universal Studio's to film "*The Creature from the Black Lagoon.*" Perry would leave in 1947 to develop another Florida underwater attraction called Weeki Wachee Springs, creating the *Newton Perry Underwater Theater* with its famous mermaids.

In 1943 the roof of the lodge was lost due to a fire. To remove the possibility of any further loss in the future, Ball had it a concrete and steel roof constructed to replace it. Ball had the river dynamited out to allow passage of his glass bottom boats, then placed a chain-link fence across the river at his property boundaries to "keep out the riff-raff." Florida environmentalists were incensed at his blocking the course of the Wakulla River. But Ball fought them in court and won saying motorboats would disturb the wildlife.

But he was also known as a conservationist, establishing the Edward Ball Wildlife Foundation in 1966 and setting aside lands preserves. He established the Wakulla Springs Wildlife Sanctuary, the Box R Sanctuary, and the Southwood Farm Sanctuary to preserve and conserve wildlife. To allow easier access to his springs he promoted the development of a road to its gates called the Bloxam Cut-off or State road 267. He also backed a state road bond proposal in the 60s to four-lane Highway 98 from Medart to Apalachicola which coincidentally ran through his land holdings, but it was defeated by the voters. Ball died in June of 1981. In 1986 the springs, lodge, and 3,000 surrounding acres were bought by the State of Florida for 9.15 million dollars another 2,000 acres were added in 2000. It now serves as the Ed Ball Wakulla Springs state park.

15

The Union Bank

The oldest bank in Florida sits on the corner of Calhoun Street and Apalachee Parkway in Tallahassee, Fl. Built in 1841 it was originally a source of loans for local planters. After the Civil War during Reconstruction times it became a Freedmen's Savings Bank for emancipated slaves. It is one of the few surviving examples of Federal commercial architecture in the state featuring blue stucco scored to look like stone.

The Union Bank, Florida Archives

16

I Ain't Got No Body!

Mausoleum of Calvin C. Phillips

Tallahassee has had its share of eccentric people and one of its most notable was Calvin C. Phillips. A building designer, Phillips was said to have designed buildings for the Chicago World's Fair and the 1890 World's Fair in Paris.

He moved to Tallahassee late in life and seemed to all to be a lonely hermit. He built a home in the All

Saint's neighborhood off of Gaines street after moving to Tallahassee around 1907. His eccentrics' were noticed in the construction of his home when he added a 30-foot clock tower. Other additions on the property included a brick building in the shape of a windmill, and a five-foot brick bird-bath and planter combination. The clock gear mechanisms was said to have been made of a wood.

**Phillips Home at 815 S. Macomb Street
from Florida Archives**

Phillips Clock Tower

Rendering of Phillips Clock Tower
by Buddy Perryman 1966

Phillips not only designed the place he lived, he also built his eternal resting place in Oakland Cemetery on the corner of Brevard and N. Bronough street. His mausoleum was the very first tomb in the new cemetery which opened in 1902-03. Local lore has it that Phillips, an elderly man bent at the waist with a waist-long beard, began constructing his crypt when he was 85 years old. When the old man needed to rest, he would go inside and lay down. When he finished two years later he had a cherry wood casket built to his specifications. He then gave a key to the mausoleum to his lawyer and friend Senator Hodges with instructions for his funeral.

Shortly thereafter, on November 10, 1919 he entered the crypt, lay down and died. His obituary noted he had a family consisting of wife and two daughters, but none came for his funeral. On the day of his funeral the flags in Tallahassee were lowered to half-mast out of respect. The mausoleum only contains the name PHILLIPS over the door. There is nothing to record his full name, date of birth, or death

It would seem that the story would end here but the quirky nature of the man developed a following among the occult. Ghost hunters were said to feel a strange coldness when walking around the crypt and others related seeing a ghost sitting atop the mausoleum. It all came to a climax 81 years later when in April of 2000 someone broke into the grave and stole Calvin C. Phillips head. The Tallahassee Police Department started an investigation that still stands open today. There were no clues to follow (though some think it was a student prank) and as of yet, no head. So the body of old Calvin calls out to no avail.

Phillips home site would be home to many different families through the years. In the late 1970s it fell into disrepair. A local preservation effort was begun but later failed and the home and clock tower were torn down in the early 1980s. No one knows what became of the clock face and mechanisms…or Phillips skull.

17

The Nautilus Foundation in Lloyd

Ok, so you say you have seen it all. Well maybe not. Outside of the fair city of Lloyd, FL is what remains of the Nautilus Foundation.

Built on a 400-acre tract and encompassing over 22,000 square feet, the buildings and the grounds of FSU Professor Francois Bucher's home is a utopian meeting place. He built it for like-minded individuals to come and contemplate life in the solitude of the North Florida woods.

Bucher wanted to construct an art castle in the woods. A medievalist and modernist, he started constructing an elongated cinderblock building in the 1980s. His idea was to create a think-tank, called *Nautilus*, that would have a lecture hall, library, art gallery and living quarters.

He based *Nautilus* on the ideas of architect and system theorist R. Buckmaster Fuller, who held the patent to the geodesic dome. Bucher embraced the beliefs that Fuller promoted that one individual could contribute to changing the world and benefit humanity.

A classically trained old world intellectual, he stored his many historical art and artifacts in his buildings. From his extensive library, to an Egyptian wood and bronze Ibis, ceremonial African masks, saints from European churches and American federalist sofas, Bucher had a little bit of everything.

Bucher's *Nautilus* Conference Center in Lloyd, Fl

Constructed with no straight walls, *Nautilus* was a monument to his architectural genius. He taught Gothic Art and Architecture at Florida State University and liked to bring his students home for seminars. Many said it was because Bucher, an avid chain-smoker, could avoid the FSU no-smoking rules at his home. Upon entering the half completed buildings, each named after a liberal art, the students would find wandering cats, butt-filled ash trays, half-filled wine bottles and coffee cups everywhere. He liked to boast that his library was better than the one at FSU and truth be known, it probably was.

Francois Bucher died in 1999 after suffering a series of strokes, no doubt brought on by his years of smoking. He is buried on the property. He bequeathed *Nautilus* and its contents to The Collins Center for Public Policy to be the Collins Nautilus Institute for Advanced Study.

The Collins Center used the property until 2013. It was later sold to a private entity. Bucher's extensive library and art collection was sold at public auction in 2012.

Made in the USA
Columbia, SC
21 July 2018